Contents

Introduction 3	Nesting and Incubation 16
The Duck Family . . 4	
Types of Ducks . . . 6	Hatching and Rearing 18
Domestic Ducks . . 10	Preening 20
Feeding 12	Flocking and Migration 22
A Duck's Life 14	Index 24

To Be a Duck

It must be fun to be a duck
and row yourself around
and race with others nip and tuck
and make a quacky sound,
and dribble water through your beak,
and wear a jacket white and sleek,
and be too waterproof to leak.

It must be fun to float and float
around and in between,
and when you're tired of being a boat
to be a submarine
and chase the minnows and the fish,
or take off with a whirry swish
and be an airplane, if you wish.
— Aileen Fisher

Jemima Puddle-Duck

Introduction

Ducks live on ponds and lakes in the country and in the city.
Some prefer fresh water, some like salt water, and some like both.

They are excellent swimmers, but on land are very poor walkers – they waddle!

Many people like ducks.
There are lots of poems written about them. Jemima Puddle-Duck is a character created by Beatrix Potter.

The Duck Family

Ducks belong to the same family
as geese and swans.
There are more than 150 different species
of duck.
Some are large.
Others are small.

Male ducks are called *drakes*.
Females are called *ducks*.
In many species, the male is more brightly
colored than the female.

Baby ducks are covered in soft, fluffy down.

All ducks share certain characteristics:

A long, flat bill, sometimes brightly colored

A long neck

Wings

Webbed feet

Tail feathers

Types of Ducks

Whistling or Tree Ducks

These ducks live in forests near ponds and streams.
They nest in trees and make a whistling sound instead of quacking.

White-faced Whistling Duck

Fulvous Whistling Duck

Shelducks

These ducks act a lot like geese.
They nest in burrows and feed by grazing.
Their feathers form colorful patterns.

Common Shelduck

Australian Shelduck

Dabbling Ducks

These ducks use their bills to filter insects and plants out of the water.

They stay in shallow water and frequently upend to feed.

They make their nests on the ground.

North American Black Duck

Australian Shoveler

Diving and Perching Ducks

Diving ducks have round bodies
that sit low in the water.
They dive under the water in search of food.

Perching ducks nest in holes in trees
and can be seen perching on branches.
Like dabbling ducks, they feed in shallow water.

Smew

Mandarin
Duck

Domestic Ducks

Muscovy Duck

Two wild species of duck have been raised as food for humans.

The Muscovy duck was tamed in South America more than five hundred years ago. The mallard was first raised in China almost two thousand years ago.

The white Pekin duck is a mallard hybrid.

The female eider duck's soft breast feathers are used to fill comforters, pillows, and jackets.

Mallard

Pekin Duck

Eider Duck

11

eeding

Ducks have three main types of feeding behavior: dabbling, diving, and grazing.

Dabbling and diving ducks feed in the water at different depths.
Dabbling ducks upend while searching for food and paddle the air with their feet.
They use their bills to filter small insects and plants from the water.
Diving ducks swim deep underwater in search of food.

Grazing ducks feed on land, eating grass and other plants.

Ducks will eat food left by humans, including grains and dried bread.
But feeding ducks can make them dependent on humans for food.
Ducks might become sick from molds on these foods, or exposed to danger from pets.

 Duck's Life

Adult ducks go through an annual cycle. Each new season brings a different set of behaviors.

In early spring, males use elaborate displays to attract a mate.
During the summer, the female raises the young, and in late summer, the adults molt their feathers.
In autumn and winter, ducks form flocks. Some species migrate to warmer regions. In the spring, the ducks return and the cycle begins again.

A DUCK'S LIFE

SPRING
- Mating
- Nesting

SUMMER
- Rearing Young
- Molting

AUTUMN
- Flocking

WINTER
- Migrating

Nesting and Incubation

The female duck usually raises and protects the young.

She makes a nest of grass or dead leaves, hidden a short distance from water, and lines it with down plucked from her breast.

The female duck lays one egg daily or every other day.
Duck eggs are pale, without markings, and vary in color, ranging from greenish blue to olive brown, cream, or white.

After laying eight to fourteen eggs, the female
sits on the eggs for about twenty-eight days
to keep them warm.
When she leaves the nest to feed,
she covers it with leaves and down
to keep the eggs warm.

Hatching and Rearing

Ducklings hatch within hours of one another, and are covered with fluffy down.
The ducklings follow their mother everywhere, and she protects them.
Sometimes she pretends to have a broken wing in order to lead predators away from the nest.

Baby ducks can walk and swim
almost immediately.
After two to three weeks, they lose their down
and begin to grow feathers.
After six weeks, the feathers are fully developed
and the ducklings are able to fly.

Preening

When people say "it's like water off a duck's back," they mean that something that has happened won't affect them, just as water won't make a duck's feathers wet.

When preening, a duck uses its bill to pick up oil from a gland at the base of its tail. It then spreads this oil over its feathers to waterproof them.

Ducks also take baths to wash off any dust or dirt that collects on their feathers. They dry themselves by flapping their wings.

Like other birds, ducks molt their old, worn feathers and grow new ones.
Unlike other birds, ducks molt all at once and are unable to fly for up to six weeks. During this time, they hide to protect themselves from predators.

Male mallard ducks lose all their bright feathers and grow a temporary "eclipse" plumage that is much less colorful.

Flocking and Migration

After molting, some ducks form into flocks that number from a dozen to a thousand birds. Often these flocks will migrate in the autumn and the winter.
Some flocks cover very long distances, up to 8,000 km (5,000 miles)!

The ducks search out warmer climates, then return at the beginning of the next spring. They lay their eggs, raise their ducklings, and repeat the cycle.

23

Index

Dabbling ducks	8, 12	Hybrids	10
Diving ducks	9, 12	Migration	14, 15
Down	4, 16, 17, 18, 19	Molting	14, 15, 21
Ducklings	4, 18-19	Nesting	6-9, 15, 16-17, 18
Eggs	16, 17, 22	Perching ducks	9
Feathers	7, 10, 19, 20, 21	Preening	20
Feeding	7, 8, 9, 12-13	Shelducks	7
Flocks	14, 15, 22	Swans	4
Flying	19	Tree ducks	6
Geese	4, 7	Whistling ducks	6
Grazing ducks	7, 13	Wings	5, 18, 20